# EARTHBOUND

## Poems

## Dee LeRoy

MUDSTONE PRESS
Earthbound
Dee LeRoy

Literary magazines and anthologies that originally published poems in this
collection are acknowledged on pages 123-124

Cover painting: Gustave Caillebotte:
The Yellow Fields at Gennevilliers

Published in the United States by Mudstone Press
ISBN-13: 978-0692264881
ISBN-10: 0692264884

What began so musically in the spring ends as a whisper.
—— E. Duensing, A.G. Millmoss, *Backyard and Beyond*

# CONTENTS

# EARTHBOUND

# MEDITATION

How long has he sat in empty peace? The pathway
smells like spring.
— Wang Wei


Emperor Huizong painted the *Five-Colored Parakeet*
with the tiniest of brush strokes
which, it was taught, enhanced revelation...

technique suggested this clear morning of early spring
when colors seem brushed over winter
with the lightest touch of spider's silk.

Here the emperor might choose for his subject
the robin singing on an oak's low limb stippled
with the pale green of new leaves...

the many-hued cardinal as she perches
among a dogwood's tiny bracts not yet white
but the light jade the emperor chose for wings.

His parakeet's breast matches the robin's
vibrating throat, the cardinal's tuft

the lone tulip a squirrel must have planted
where the fence sections meet:

1

harmony that will disappear as crimson flowers fill in
yield in turn to blue. Soon robin song will end
with new robins. Toad song, with new toads.

Caterpillars just hatched will grow into their hunger
or be eaten. And from one brown recluse whose egg
hangs in an idle shoe many will scatter.

So the student of peace walking spring's path
practices the art of breathing—filling but not holding
as an ear receives music and remains empty.

# I

# CHERRY, OAK, WOODPECKER

In a watery landscape that might be Monet's
our new spring lacks the usual crisp edges.

Cherry trees are heavy as ever with blossom
as perfectly posed.

Yet pinks leak into whites and into the gray of mist
where even the round sun loses shape.

On such days it is not this season's petals I want to admire
but their anchor—

the thin skeletons rooted in earth or the massive trunks
of trees whose flowers are too high, too small to see—

the oak on whose hollow limb a woodpecker taps
calling for a mate:

sharp, hard sound hopeful and clear.

# FIREWATER

I took it in tiny sips, feeling its burn
then slipped into daydream

hearing your voice
say how the drink began

with apples: fruits of Cézanne's table
so yellow, so red

so hot they would ignite the house
if the cloth were not blue.

*

You told me once: even if I asked it
you would not walk through fire

my expectations hovering
flaming hoops.

Yet you walked through water
the day we married, vowing
rain meant luck.

*

This morning even before you left
the radio announced injury
along your route.

All day I listened
as water exploded on the house.

And though I know now you are safe
fear washes back

through that faulty valve whose uneven
rhythm keeps time with rain.

*

You were away when the tree branch
pierced the roof.
It had the scent of burning wood

and it lodged like a stake
over our bed, dripping water.

# BROADKILL BEACH

August

We lie on the altar
of the sun

near remains
of those the ocean chose
to sacrifice this day—

flattened medusa
on the sand

*Limulus*
already decayed—

wary
of this star of ours
the more for knowing

half its life is past
and tempers flare
in middle age.

It will die rudely
we are told

boiling first
the unsuspecting sea

devouring its planets
in mortal rage.

Already it presses
its small demands:

granting sight, destroying it
if the eye stares back
too hard

warming us
until we burn.

# SILTSTONE

Probably weathering and normal fracturing,
not imprints of anything, probably in a
siltstone...
— Naturalist Center, Smithsonian Institution

Grain by grain the ocean built it
abandoned and retrieved it
sent it now to shore in that wet band
of shells and stones the tide leaves–

treasures of the beach: practical
like the clam shell for ashes, colored pebbles
for a fishbowl in the den

and transcendent
like the shark's tooth for luck or this rock
alone terra cotta and gray pressed with shapes
of butterfly wings and feathers.

Once it would have been thought fossil
worn as amulet, taken as devil's trick.
Now they say it is merely itself:

stone too flat to roll landward
too weak to resist water's muscle
the creases and scars on its weathered face
accidental symbols of flight.

# GLASS

A man on the shore before history
walks the smooth surface
which shattered cuts through flesh:

lightning on sand—
earth's matter, sky's heat.

Babylonians left the recipe on stone.
Romans valued it as gold.

We seek our face there
give it our breath

find heart or soul
as if the transparent vase feels
emptiness

or the anniversary paperweight
wills itself to sit
solid as the marriage vow

breakable as trust.

Glass cups sing under a child's
wet finger, a musician's hand.

Mozart wrote for glass.
Jefferson praised its music.

Yet others blamed the sound
for madness and death

hearing perhaps
behind the sweet harplike tone
a persistent note of terror

a mosquito's screech as it flies
past the ear
hungry for blood.

# EVIDENCE FOR STRINGS

> If string theory is right, the microscopic fabric
> of the universe is a richly intertwined multidi-
> mensional labyrinth within which the strings of
> the universe endlessly twist and vibrate, rhyth-
> mically beating out the laws of the cosmos.
> — Brian Greene, *The Elegant Universe*

If it is true that strings form the universe
and all we know of it—nothing
but shards of vibrating space and time—
we will ask ourselves surrounded by the echo
how we missed the clues.

On the wall of a French cave: a man dressed as bison
plays mouth bow—single string resonating in himself
with all the magic

of Apollo's lyre lulling the gods of Olympus to forget
or the lyre of Orpheus that moved trees, tamed beasts
altered rock, turned a river, reversed death—

something we still pray for, in chorus or alone
with the cords of our voices.

The biblical David plucked a harp to release Saul
from evil. Listening, Saul, bent forward
wiped his eye with a velvet curtain pulled
from the dark. So Rembrandt painted it:
harp's music, David's innocence
Saul's fugitive peace nothing but thin, threadlike
strokes of color.

Van Gogh wrote to his brother of calm
and pure music, the secretive vibration of tones
then built earth and sky and all he knew of them
with twisting ropes of paint

as later Klee would play the violin
before he took up his brush. He painted
moonlit grass—a line of silver blades
dotted with yellow birds—clef with notes
that could sing if they wanted to—and he wrote:

*I am closer than usual to the heart of creation*
*yet far from close enough.*

# VIOLIN

Lodged in each home between bookshelf
and wall, the case has grayed
brass latch blackened.

And if, inside, the bridge is dark
or pegs no longer grip,
the neck and shoulders still rest snug
on their velvet bed:

instrument laid here young
hushed for half its life

as if asleep and waiting
in forest's perfume
for someone to break the curse.

Forty years the scored rosin
has remained unmoved in its pocket
lies there now

though once it powdered the bow
white as the wigs of Louis Quinze

(who might have seen the violin's wood
living).

But the bow forty years hanging
in the case's lid, so formal in its mute
bowing toward the strings

has lately come apart:
hair separated from wood

fallen across the violin's rounded belly
as if exhausted by long restraint

and straining now to find the pulse
of trapped music

the way one presses an ear to a lover's chest
when sleep makes no sound
listening for beats.

# MUSIC ROOM

The student waits
hands chilled by room and weather.

*Why am I here?* A silent refrain.

She stares at a poster
absent or unseen before—Vivaldi
violin to chin, holding his bow
just as she has been trying to hold her own

just as he taught the orphaned girls
at La Pietà to hold theirs
this ailing composer-priest rumored
to have walked out of his Masses
to note any melodic inspiration

though in truth he was trying
to catch breath or relieve a pain
in his heart.

In the portrait gold tones fill his space.
They hug his hands, instrument, and music:
warmth that once noticed also seeps
into the room where the poster hangs

like the low sun in this maestro's native city
warming the stone houses
against the gray waters of canal and sea.

# SOUL OF WATER

The four categories of souls in whose
dreams fire, water, air, or earth predominate
show themselves to be markedly different.
— Gaston Bachelard


Water governed Monet's dreams
called him to Atlantic
to Mediterranean

to the Seine at Argenteuil
and at Giverny
where it meets the Epte.

He built a boat, traveled the river
with easel and paints
stopping when a scene caught his eye.

And he brought his soul of water
onto land, rendering the flow
of weather and time

as they washed
over haystack and cathedral.

Poppies drifted down meadow.

Skirts bobbed on the lawn
where a woman sat to read a book.

And even the poplars along the river
seemed soaked
in water's reflection

to be distorted, perhaps erased
by a wind gust
or the stroke of a duck's webbed foot.

# VISIT TO BRITTANY

We saw the houses from the gate, clouded windows
rimmed red with inlaid brick

stone facades rich in browns and grays exposing skins
of pale cement, like robes of an old woman that fall open
though she does not know it.

At the largest house: your aunt waiting—small, gnarled
glad for guests, mind as filled with family stories as the houses
with their stores of farm tools, furniture, linens.

Soon she was telling again how your father was born
in the smallest house, lived in the others built for new babies
until he sailed from the nearby coast

how an uncle borrowed from his brothers and wealthy
did not pay the debt, how a cousin's wife in love
with a handyman followed him to another town:

news nearly as old as the kitchen clock, town's name
etched on its face, ticking still.

Listening we could imagine aromas from the cold soup pot
the stern voice of your grandmother—whose late face all agree
you have borrowed—

calling to the eight she bore here (your aunt practicing for us
the names, the years of birth and death).

When we spoke, we asked about the newer generations—
the cousins near Paris. About the cherry tree in the courtyard:
when it was planted, why a main branch was torn away.

We did not say even to each other how fumes from the city's
traffic drifted that autumn over the gate, across the burnt grass
into the one window left open

or how far you had to bend when we arrived
to pass through the kitchen door.

# NOVEMBER PASSAGE

Nohèdes, France

This autumn, they say,
the bare trees seem grayer
peaks thicker with snow.

Harvest in, the old villagers
take up other chores—

canning fruit
slating roofs, oiling gates—

animated by anticipation:

awaiting the sheep
that every year appear
on their way downslope
to warmer fields.

They moan
about the expected guests—

how they'll clog the paths
dirty the streets
for the last fall flies—

while their faces soften
with affection deep
as the unspoken fear

that one year
the sheep will not come.

So restless they are
for the annoying beasts
that all day call to each other

all night cloud the air
with their damp, warm smell.

# REGRET

You kick it
off the porch
but it returns
soon enough
whiskers twitching
all the more eager
for admission.
So you let it in
name it
nurture it
learn to live
with the purring of it
heavy and warm
in your lap
its hooked claws
kneading your heart
with affection.

# YOUNG GIRL WHO LOOKS INTO A MIRROR

and vows to seek a perfect face
I beg you:

Delay the permanent cut. Come first
into the public garden and explore.

For beauty's sake

they have killed the geese and deer
pulled up the scruffy brush

though in fall its lavender berries
were the garden's special color.

They have filled the pond where frogs
once filled their throats with song

replaced them with daffodils—lovely, mute
identical to so many nearby.

If you stay long enough you will begin
to miss the pluck of thorn and scum.

Look. Here in bloom apart from the rest
is a pink camellia

carefully tended, perfectly placed.
It should lift the heart.

But its flowers rot at the edges, are fast shed.
And the shrub from which they fall

will soon stand plain and alone
after a blush that could not last.

# BLACK BALLOON

Mother and child
on a bench
at the zoo—

the mother blowing up
a black balloon, child
transfixed on that darkness

expanding like the universe
but in rhythm
with this mother's breath:

expanding faster with time
as the universe
is said to

stars like ourselves
leaving their moment of birth
with increasing speed.

The balloon burps
as it is knotted.
The child laughs.

When she takes it from her mother
her fingers bend
the thin skin of space.

# THREE ELEPHANTS

Their arrival was unquestioned:
Three elephants thin as paper—
ruby, amber, green—

paced the floor
where Golden books and puzzles lay.
They sat on bed or chair.

Nights they slid beneath a rug
reappeared at dawn

to spend the day with stories:
the slow puppy
in trouble for being late...

little engine whose heart
was brave...

the shape of Kentucky—favorite
puzzle piece—where soon, they said
they would go for a long vacation.

Past and future
had no interest then.

We did not wonder
how life is freed by lightning
from gas and dust, by sperm from egg...

how color springs from dewdrops
after a strike of morning sun...

even how red, yellow, and green
playmates are born
from the light of a child's eye

to be called back with a blink—
as the cloud recalls the rainbow.

# RIDING LESSON

The horses were led out
one by one:

Man o' War's
granddaughter, flammable
as a match

muscular browns and blacks
with white diamonds
between their eyes

the chunky mare last:
short, gray, with wispy
black mane, square-angled
as a mule.

She walked the stable's path—
letting the others trot or gallop by—

stopping often to eat leaves
or stretch her neck down
for dandelions.

The instructor beat her into
faster gaits so her Scouts
could get the badge

but soon she would be
walking again, up the path
toward a favorite stand
dark with trees

pupils brilliant as moons
catching the subtle light.

# LETTER FOR A GRADUATION

As you leave your home,
your strip of beach, for more study—

medicine, perhaps,
in case the acting fails—

you are practical
and zany as you were
when you took the red-nosed reindeer
from the toy heap

called it Toto, cast it
in *The Wizard of Oz.*

Each Tuesday, we played
at something (your mother tending
laundry, dinner, nerves)—

Wonderland, Pooh Corner,
the home where Mary Poppins worked...

We dressed you, Cinderella,
in your mother's shoes
my magic wand waving
until, last minute

you offered a sequined scarf
pulled me with you to the den
sure there would be *two highnesses*
at the ball.

*People get different faces, don't they?*
you asked at age three.
At five, you got a heavy face.

Confidence waned
family changed states...
Then you, yourself, grew up.

Now you graduate well prepared
knowing ogres, princes
yellow brick road

how sand shifts and water kills more
than bad witches.

You know the world you go to
can be false as the Wizard
more twisted than the logic
of a playing card at croquet:

a place to get lost in
to lose one's head.

*Off with her head*, roared the Queen.
But Alice stood her ground

and soon she was home again
head intact, running off to tea.
Remember that.

And remember me.

# THE LADY AND THE
# UNICORN

Musée National du Moyen Age—Thermes de
Cluny, Paris

*I. Museum*

Rooms harbor what Medieval hands could craft
for worship and war. Chivalry, conquest, inquisition
turned cold. Faded threads, iron rusted, stone
becoming dust

and in this pale setting the red tapestries
holding animals, leaves, flowers and fruit—
what earth offers to sight, smell, taste, hearing, touch

to the lion and unicorn and to the lady they honor
on her green-blue island of only slight restraint.

*II. Lion*

He brings to this Eden the world outside—
sweat of combat for power and gold—
as he scans garden's horizon

ready to defend the lady
who delights in music and food
surrounded by the scent of blossoms.

His task is great, face nervous
fierce, excited, insane.

If ever appetite should trump duty here
this hunter would not starve,
his quick eyes already taking census

of rabbit and goat. Even the lady
and her servant would be fair game.

But the tender unicorn with narwhal tusk
horse's hooves, a tail not unlike
the lion's own

has appeared out of fable
and eludes the lion's notice entirely.

### III. Lady

Whoever set her here adored her, mirrored her spirit
in jaguar, partridge, duck.

Even the maid's face is hers, changes panel to panel
as hers does, clothes and jewels simpler versions of her own.

All is in balance: leaves evenly spaced, hunter and prey
suspended at peace

music and aroma contained by the demands of good taste.

Still, her eyes show strain: constant sun, the dread
of garden's fall exhaust her. Soon she will return to her life

afraid only of failing him who had her woven into a world
where everything is good.

*IV. A Mon Seul Désir*

She removes her jewels, prepares to enter the tent
of love and death. To go is her one desire.
Living is what matters, after all.

Behind her the garden's impossible order will shatter—
oranges rot, fox reduce duck and partridge
to piles of feathers.

The dog will follow his mistress, resume tugging
at her hem. The maid, too, will walk behind her
growing slowly older and more prone to mood.

The lion after having his fill will flee to forest
while his image rides to war etched in soldiers' armor.

But the unicorn if the lady wills it will remain with her
affectionate, unchanged, a companion to dailiness
cantering in her kitchen garden, napping on her lap.

*V. Unicorn*

Whitest white, tender, pure, the one
who makes the senses' pleasures sweet

who gazes at the lady—and at us—as if to lighten
the weight of our clothes, erase shadow from our flesh.

What are earth's riches to this creature
but objects of love?

Lady, keep the unicorn beside you even when husband
or child distracts. A wife, a mother must nurture

myth—the being without guile or greed or pain
the only one whom death cannot touch.

II

# THE DOCTOR'S VISIT

after Jan Steen

Even before he takes
fluids and pulse
he knows it is the heart
that is sick—

his patient slumped, mute
chilled in her thick velvet jacket
hand on forehead, eyes wet

the old father sitting in shadow
reading the latest intercepted letter.

The window is shuttered.
Nothing in this house is green.

On the wall Venus and Adonis
embrace a last time
before he joins the hunt
that will kill him

while in smaller frame
a clownlike man grins

as the doctor and the housemaid
might, who now scarcely contain
their amusement
over the mundane drama
of love.

The gold clock's armored soldier
lifts a hammer
to strike another hour

and even the dog lying at her feet
begins to signal betrayal
lifting his head, sniffing the air
for something new.

On the floor a red-cheeked child
turns from her, sets a new arrow
in his tiny bow.

# THE PEASANT WEDDING BANQUET

after Pieter Bruegel the Elder

Vows have been spoken
and a hungry crowd has walked
from village church to barn's large room
pressing toward the table
where early arrivals already carve
rabbit, grouse, round loaves of bread.

Pie is served with garnish of cream
mead passed in pitchers
tall as a man's calf.
Fat children lick fingers.
Bagpipers finger chanters—the usual
lusty songs.

If landowner is ruler and judge
here he abandons that role.
Among the warmed guests, gums bared
appetites large as the muscles in their backs
he is the one seated at picture's edge ignored
by all except the birdlike daughter beside him.

Even the two whose union was just blessed
matter little to the celebration:
The groom hides...
gone off perhaps to discuss the coming harvest...
or mingles here unnoticed
one of the men with belted knives.

The bride sits wooden—
medieval saint—
hands folded, eyes closed
crown like halo over long, loose hair
ruddy cheeks sole hint that room's heat
begins to consume her.

Tomorrow when she wakes
she will be one more village wife
soon with child and worn as the soil
she will help her husband work.
At the next feast, in her matron's bonnet
we will hardly know her.

# PORTRAIT OF MADAME CHARDIN

after Jean Siméon Chardin,

Her husband was a private man
preferred home
to drawing room or café

as Paris spun
around him—

the gilded carriages
beggars in rags

Louis XV under spell
of mistress
losing the Empire

and news from America
beginning to stir
revolution already in the air.

\*

He chose still life
simple interior

while others more honored
painted myth—
Diana or the Muses;

religion—wicked son punished: canvas
of pain: a lesson.

And they said he lacked imagination
painting only what he could see.

*

In the Salon of 1740
on a small canvas he would later give
to the King

a child is at prayer
on a seat she has outgrown

sister and mother

(who has stopped serving
evening soup to listen)

joining her
with their eyes.

Earlier she was playing the drum
that hangs from the chair
the flute lying on the floor

will play them again.

But now it is time
for the softer sound of grace:

plates are full; the soup thick—
potato, carrot, leek, steaming;

the chair's upholstery
is fat with stuffing;

and, beyond,
a pan on the mantel is shining
like a moon that might
when time begins again

rotate slowly around the room.

\*

He was in his seventies
when he switched to portrait—
pastel instead of oil—

drawing his wife like himself
without the customary wig
or formal dress

their heads wrapped in similar
white, blue-bowed caps
against the Paris chill.

They had married thirty years earlier—
widow, widower—
both said to be honest
and kind.

He could not deny her age—
the pallor, the folds of flesh
the thinning of her lips

which—corners slightly upturned—
seemed to approve him.

Nor could he dismiss
the hazel eyes—steady and clear
as when they first met—

settled now on his own sunken face
seeming to bless him.

He had spent a life
observing the heart of things

and has turned his gaze
this once
just on her.

# INSULATION

November 2001

The old roof is being ripped away
fiberglass stuffed among the rafters
debris tossed into the yard.

The carpenter's footsteps
his pounding and scraping
vibrate in the walls.

We've been lucky, you and I
under the old shingles

and though it is time to repair
years of slow damage

you with your passion
for taking things apart delight
too much in this tearing up

this insulating of a drafty house
from which for years
we've shared our warmth
with the wind.

You're not alone in this fixation:
hardware stores report
brisk sales

and according to the news
Americans are "cocooning"—

building up their houses
constructing defenses.

Instead, I've been scouting
the perimeter, clearing spaces
for spring gardens:

uprooting ivy, letting leaves
as they fall pile thick
over newly bared soil
with its resting seeds and roots.

After decades trying to force
delphinium and rose
whose blooms are greedy for light

I'm adjusting my eyes to shadow—
blue hydrangea
fern's curved spine.

I know now that the four o'clocks
wait until seven to open
and will meet them on their terms.

On our cracked sidewalk
a woolly bear
plump with summer's plantain

models its lush coat
moving with a certain
slow swagger

though it doesn't know its future
any more than we can predict
winter

with our opposite readings
of its stripe.

If it dodges rake and beak
it will find space under leaves
to rest awhile
gather strength for change.

And if spring comes
calling for wings
it will have time enough then
to spin a loose cocoon

and get down to the work
of growing them.

# FLOWERS IN A GLASS VASE

after Abrosius Bosschaert the Elder

Tulip, forget-me-not
lily of the valley
fritillary, rosemary and rose—
they tower over the vase
glossy faces lit with color
staged as if by Wagner.

For they are plucked
from different seasons
born of time
but without its scent:
pact with the devil—perhaps
that butterfly in shadow.

Even the fallen pansy seduces
elegant dying diva
her last scene preserved here
all actors on stage
Red Admiral holding the score
between his great closed wings.

# PLANTING TULIPS

Buried deep in the make-up of the flamboyant,
cultivated tulips that fill flower shops in spring
must be the ghostly genes of their wild cousins.
— Anna Pavord


On Saint Vitus Day, spring 1389
Lazar, Prince of Serbs
was killed by Turks at Kosovo
on a battlefield so strewn
with brightly turbaned heads
it was compared to a bed of tulips.

Today we planted cousins
of those Eastern flowers
tamed long ago to European taste
and so alluring
the wealthy burghers of Holland
lost their heads: single bulbs
for the price of houses, gardens inflated
by reflection in mirrored gazebos
flower portraits painted in oil
on canvas or wood.

The Dutch artist Jan van Goyen
died insolvent. Not from painting
tulips. He collected them—
in one purchase paying
fifty guilders
his *Picture of Judas*
and a work by Ruijsdael
for just six bulbs
the money alone more than a bricklayer's
annual wage.

Even the prosperous could not dictate
every variation,
coating garden soil with paint
to force flames onto feathered petals—
the coveted bloom,
genetic break commanding
the highest price—
though it was virus brought by aphids
that rendered the design
a secret tulips held for centuries

as we hold in ourselves
a wildness that broken loose
inflames us
to trade gold for dreams
bomb a bus or market
shoot a neighbor because
long ago our princes fought.

*Burning Heart, Temple of Beauty...*

the well-bred names
carry the old tales with them—
lust, jealousy, murder
curled white this late October
in their tear-shaped, copper-skinned bulbs.

In spring when they sprout
drop their outermost veils
burn our eyes with their colors
so many together on a tiny plot
one will grow amid the bright flowers
dark as their afterimage—

*Queen of Night*

red turned black
like an old wound.

# VERDUN

They called it Hell:

a million maimed or killed—
odor for years

over ground so swollen
no crop would grow.

Yet nine decades later
the earth is lush:

green leaves low and close
with colza—sulfur's yellow
like flame among them.

Mustard family...

Along the main road east
from Metz

lined with graves marked
"German" or "French"
the colza, too,
could seem memorial

though it likely signals
only that spring has come
with its usual mission

and no use for labels.

What do the blossoms know
of the gas that shares
their family name

their darker foreign
designation: rape

their brimstone color
their own rotten smell?

# RUBY

If cast into the water the ruby
communicated its heat to the liquid,
causing it to boil...
— George Kunz, *The Curious Lore
of Precious Stones*

Stone of summer, look
how the season assumes your reds—

hummingbird throat, columbine's bell
impatiens spread over the bed's dark floor.

You are set in breastplate
necklace and flesh to guard from harm.
But your fire offers no such promise.

See how the carmine hibiscus, favorite of bees
makes fists of its petals at dusk
clenched like hands of children
disturbed in dream

how the cardinal's crimson feathers
piled by nocturnal hunter
bleed into the sidewalk after rain

how war's planet, too, bears your tint
of blood.

Days hang on.
Yet even the large, ruby sun
finally drops away, bowing to night.

The wise bee renders ruby black.

# WHEAT FIELD WITH CROWS

Auvers-sur-Oise, July 1890

Color of mourning and madness
space beyond sun
black was always at the edge
of Van Gogh's vision—
around tree, face, church, chair—
vessel for what he made bright.

But when illness grew as thick
as the paint he pressed on canvas
black took wing:
crows between the grain's gold
and cobalt sky over a green road
lost midfield.

Along Montrose Road
in a stand of trees
crows gather daily like this
(birds known for remembering
for stealing what is bright
for their nests).

When a friend sickened
and asked to see those crows
once more

we sat in a car on a winter afternoon
watched as they arrived in thousands
wailing, drumming their wings
and later as suddenly departed

swirls across dusk
mocking negative of stars.

# VETERANS DAY

A forester marks for cutting
the bent oak—

root rot, trunk
that turns to powder—

here since the war
that gave the Day its date

and tall already
when, another war later,
the house was built beside it.

So tall the bark
is what we know best—
wolf spider's lookout,
camp for beetle and moth.

We've heard the gray squirrel
and crow, posted higher,
as they issued orders
across the yard

mouse or vole as it crept
under cover of fallen leaves

acorns that popped
like muffled gunshot.

We've taken much
for granted—

shade, leaves' breath
support as we climbed
the sidewalk steps—

so absence is what we'll notice
more: how the yard
thins again

like the old companies
that used to reunite this day
fewer and fewer left standing.

# HOUSE SPARROWS

These are loud and crowded
neighbors one learns to ignore

descended from an English group
come by boat to Brooklyn

when humans, too,
were docking there
in similar browns and grays.

Songbirds without song
they breed under our eaves

flock at our feet
cleaning beneath tables
gleaning from the pavement's cracks

though sometimes one
among them gives
a grave or lonely sign:

the mother flying a tissue streamer
toward a nest above the road

or on that road a fallen chick
wings still waving
tiny in its loose coat of feathers.

# A RIVER BACK

When they came to America
Celia and her sister
spoke to one another
in the new language as soon
as they could learn it...

though seventy years later chose
their native tongue to remember
gathering mushrooms in the forest
washing clothes in the river
near the village of their youth.

Their talk flowed
toward their graves—
yet splashed on the way
against shrieks of mirth
as it carried them back

to the perfect landscape
of a home their parents warmed
with what the trees could give
and the soldiers fired,
for a while, elsewhere.

# KITTNER'S STORE

Weldon, NC

Here in spring the women chose
floral prints, Easter bonnets
new white shoes

children in fall found boots and coats
and all year men considered Sunday
suits and ties

while ceiling fans hummed
over the *yes-sir* and *yes-ma'am*
of polite Southern talk.

It stands nearly empty now
on the town's main street
attended by a few it nurtured

like the hollow tree on a nearby road
that dies in the company of some
from its generations of birds.

When it goes the uncles likely will resettle
leaving the town

in one way at least
as it was a century before:
without us.

Already a eulogy was written
for a local paper. The family plans
a reunion in another state.

And yesterday my mother told me
a dress from my closet, smelled

"like the clothes at Kittner's"—
mothballs and leather—

as if my house
two hundred miles from the family store
were one of its offspring

assuming its traits
as often children acquire those
of a parent passing away.

# ALIGNMENTS

May 10, 2002

The five appeared from out of town
without formal invitation
to honor the eighty-fifth year
of their eldest brother—

have aligned themselves
at the restaurant's long table

as once, children, they sat
for the noon meal
in the house on Sixth Street.

Talk turns them back there
to a remaining question:


Who was it that died at their parents' table
just after the first of them was born
(event grown-ups mentioned only
in whisper or by slip of tongue)?

*I thought it was Dr. Gordon,* one says,
describes how she never was at that table
without a shiver she took
for Dr. Gordon's ghost.

But her brothers remember
the doctor: home from a trip abroad
and in the mood to show off
telling their immigrant father
he really must visit Europe sometime

the father answering softly
he had been there already.

*Then it must have been
the brother-in-law of Dr. Todd.* Heads nod
reminding someone of a story
with a punch line that causes tears
in three who inherited their mother's laugh.

From the old house they had spun off
in different directions

settled into their educations, wars
families, jobs.

Paths were set, visits brief—
in groups with children
then children's children:

noisy, unsettled, safe
from gravity and whimsy.

Today the past envelops them
thick with the scent
of their mother's bread

their faces lit reflections
of common DNA.


When they part at dusk—
some to dates with nearby children
others toward home—

at least one old question
is answered: it was the brother-in-law
of Dr. Todd.

*Clear weather,* they say to one another.
*Take care. It was a nice day.*

In the night sky five of the sun's planets
align themselves with Earth
near enough to be seen
without lenses:

conjunctions that have not occurred
for decades.

The planets differ in substance
spin and time
in weather and force of attraction

but gathered here—
reflecting the light
the pull, of a common star—
they seem familiar

close
even as they separate
and move alone across the dark.

# III

# SEPTEMBER

Each year the tilt toward fall
surprises:

Earth's night turning from its Milky Way
toward dimmer worlds

sapphire sky pale to dark
pooling over hills

tinting aster and ironweed
the last morning glory whose indigo petals
open around a star.

A tree that looks green drops a yellow leaf
and afternoon's blue deepens around it

as if what is lost remains close
to cushion descent.

One by one the days shorten.

# THE OLD HOUSE

I tell you the past is a bucket of ashes.
— Carl Sandburg


Midday along a silent street
the house in thick gray paint
displays itself

like an old snapshot—
dulled image of the white brick
and black trim it once had:

clean look of the fifties—
decade itself black and white
with its races separate
ideas unchallenged.

Still, the street then had accents
of color—fresh grass and roses.

School out, color would also seep
into the children's faces

as we rode up that street and down
on bikes and skates.

A violinist lived next door
whose father-in-law
when he paid a visit
set an easel on the porch
painted orange zinnias.

A block away: three young sisters
at tag in red shorts or blue
already carrying the gene
for early cancer

and a blond bride from France
who would be the last
of the neighbors to remain.

After we left
all of them faded quickly
in recollection

while more slowly
they themselves went gray
lawns paled

and the old house became
what memory had already made of it—
color of soot

as if a cold heart casts deadly spells
even on brick
can turn even that to ash.

# BONNARD'S PEACHES

Cousins of the rose

their tones filled his palette:
landscapes and rooms dense with sun

and the same yellow-orange-red
lightly blended in the skin
of his naked Marthe

model-mistress-wife.

Sometimes the fruits alone
were the models:

1916 plump with juice
leaves green
the white cloth splashed with pink

or 1941 leaves blue and sparse
peaches shriveled, dark
barely touching...

as if the same ones had sat
twenty-five years on a single canvas

losing vigor
while the painter's own had ebbed.

*Peaches are astonishing.*
*This year I was much struck by them*
he said in '42

moved perhaps less by beauty
than by nostalgia or decay.

By then his country was in another war.
Marthe was dead.

He was seventy-five
and even the table's cloth
had lost its blush.

# THE YELLOW FIELDS AT GENNEVILLIERS

*after Gustave Caillebotte*

He has left Paris
and the two-faced building
that sits like a hungry god

while men and women
in latest fashion
walk the avenues

each in the bubble
of his or her umbrella.

And now he has planted his easel
here, in the colorful fields
near Gennevilliers:

rust, ocher, and green—
low crops so lush

that of the earth beneath
they reveal only
its perfume.

On canvas, brush in hand
he leads our gaze
toward the horizon

blue-gray silhouette
of a town
diminished by distance

where in dim rooms
of a stone lycée
children are taught
to reach for the stars.

Then he invites us
to turn back. To leave
school and museum behind

and be happiest here
as he is—
where the nearest star
reaches down to him

where the hum of bees
muffles a steeple's chimes
as they try to mark the hours.

# BLUE FLOWER

You come upon a wildflower
out of season:

chicory—
so common that in summer
you might not notice one plant

as now you do walking along the road
in cloudy autumn.

At first you think it a dream
this asterisk of color
petals delicately wrinkled around the eye

but you sink deep
into this reservoir of summer sky—
its singular shade of blue.

You notice the stem's slight bend
the wilt of a leaf

and how the flower seems to grow larger
as you look.

Though once you might have thought
to uproot it
or cut it for display

now you want only
that its short life be light.

You wish it could know you are glad
for the touch of a flower
in your own out-of-season heart

warmth of summer shared
as you stand in the cold fall air.

# FLAT RUN

The feeling [of enchantment] comes
from living in two dimensions of time: the fast
time of...living things...and the slow time
of the earth... — Gloria M. Hammack


We begin our visit on the porch
facing out, name what we can see:

Queen of the Meadow
head in silhouette
with butterflies and bees
landing, escaping, landing again

a ridge beyond, more solid and still
though streams continue loud
in their sculpting.

As we move inside
talk turns to people—

C. with the bad eye who never smiled...
N. who told us she had already seen
a cherry tree in bloom
felt no need to seek out another...

R. in whose yard near here
we camped for a dulcimer convention—
that loud adventure

which led you later to this land so free
of human noise.

We count, fill in the years late
around your table, note often how fast
those years have passed.

Yet, here, for that instant
our lives seem fixed as the mountain
pressing its memories of fern

baring the fossils in their turn
after rain.

# SAGUARO

I am rough and plain,
flesh pocked
with old nests of flickers

though these last years
I allow myself
in season

crowns of white flowers
beads—the scarlet fruit.


Born under a paloverde
decades gone

I have moved
only as far as I can sway

while the unfamiliar
strays toward me—

car hum
air's acrid taste
knife slash, bullet.

My visitors, young
running, flying
seem unaffected:

Elf owl and mouse
scratch as they cool
against my flesh

bat, honeybee drink
from the night blossoms

coyote, pig, Papago, Pima
harvest the fruit.


What seeds they leave
I offer the land—

to be swallowed or nurtured
as it wills...


And I raise my limbs
toward the sky...

Here one century
I will not outlast the next

will likely die as most do—
rotted, lightning-torn
uprooted by wind…

Or—maybe—
death will puddle around me
from rare, hard rain.

Then I shall gulp it
expand beyond
my fluted body

and sated split open
for the sun to take me.

# SNOWMAN

turned from the road
toward a creek

running cold yet unfrozen
near trees beyond the house.

I circled him, faced him
grinned at his quartz pebble smile.

Though he could not tip his hat
I knew he wanted to.

"Watch your back," I said
though I saw he had no ears.

The carrot nose twitched slightly
as if he chuckled at my wit.

Only the eyes betrayed
more somber meditation

their marbled glass
reflecting sky-trees-me

all like the creek in our flowing.

There I thought I saw
the snowman's heart.

I recalled how in summer
I contemplate the soil

all it produces, all it reclaims.

"Water to water," I whispered
touching the snowman's face

lifting my hand quickly
as a drop began down his cheek.

# NEW YEAR'S EVE

The night served its warnings—
bare fists of trees balanced over the roof
breath freezing in our wake
repeating prediction
of a new year's first storm.

The home of friends
warmth escaping an open door
welcomed us as cave fires
must have greeted hunters
returning from dark forest.

Inside, paella cooked—sea and spice.
A furnace breathed
with the steady rhythm of sleep.
And in the hearth a log fire
like one that might have thawed
a hunter's bones.

Over hors d'oeuvres, over shrimp, clam
chicken, rice, talk flowed mouth to ear
as wine poured bottle to glass—
*...in Maine camping...pneumonia...baby girl!...*
*how many now?...begged her to join us...*
*lost without him—*

reminders that celebration
if honest is bittersweet.

Still, midnight as we raised champagne
let it spark in our hands
we seemed shielded against coming winds
our pointed hats, loud horns fierce with magic
to keep us safe.

# MILLENNIUM

## January 1, 2000

Weeks before we arrived at the triple-ringed gate
of the new year the night in its silk
seemed ready for the party—

for the pop and hiss of fireworks already waiting
backstage to crack the lock.

A sequined cloak hanging in a closet
glittered prematurely whenever the door was opened

and even Mendelssohn
unwinding in the room's yellow light
was like a streamer flowing
toward the upcoming celebration.

If, in the rush, we arrived at the new century—
the new millennium—twelve months early
who can blame us?

if we stormed in, eyes open, looking for omen?

or if, this morning, we breakfast on hope, that gift
of Pandora: three places set with zeros
like bowls of new snow blank and blinding?

# GINKGO

Tablet or capsule: three
each day to open memory

though not so wide
you slide in too deep
dwell there.

*

Of healing plants
*Ginkgo biloba* is oldest:

wood brushed by brontosaurus
leaves torn, ground to paste
in the reptile's gizzard of stones

of its Family, alone to survive
the Ice.

*

South of the Yangtze river, east
all men since the beginning
would have known

*the tree with leaves*
*like duck feet*:

two hundred million years there
where temples now stand.

Bells toll, monks rise
ginkgos thrum:
bone and wood ringing.

*

Pest, rot, dust, fume...
Little disturbs it
along the New World's noisy streets.

Its trunk is rough and furrowed.
Seeds when they fall are foul
as rancid butter.

But this late November
when poplar and oak are bald
ginkgo's crown is full

each splayed leaf
yellow fan modestly waving.

# FERNS

We gather in clumps at garden's edge
like silent old men who meet in the park.

Under lilac and redbud our fiddleheads unfurl
fanfare barely noticed.

We arch fronds toward earth or back, beckoning.
No one comes: roses bloom nearby.

A wood thrush sings the cry of dinosaurs
tempered now to perfect harmony

humid echo of giants falling soft around us
as each note breaks across time

loses itself in the trees.

# WAKING

Shadow moves behind the eye.
A lemon, a violin

unite in a thought
then sink into a black river.

A dead friend is digging a garden.
A red lacquer boat fills with snow.

The moon leaves a print
on the white morning sky.

# DOGWOOD

Limbs are bare
where days before
they wore rubied sleeves.

Midnight has passed.
Coach is pumpkin.
Mice run to gather seed.

And word goes forth
that winter knocks
at every gate
bearing a crystal slipper.

# THIRD BEAGLE

Cindy has escaped again
runs through yards
tail up, nose parting the grass.

She looks back
as he points his cane, limps
in her direction:

*Cin-Dee, Cin-Dee*:
his third beagle.

Her tricolor coat, hanging ears might be
those of the late Sammy I or II
but their faces showed

only adoration
while hers—brow bearing down—
hints mischief.

For hours each day
they walk, master and dog tethered
to one another—

for him a routine grown harder
with each successive pet.

His shoulders have stooped
steps stiffened.
His commands have turned coarse

more severe as block after block
he scolds:

*Cin-Dee, No!*

I imagine him a Frank or Joe
in his white tee, loose slacks

and—from the bark of his voice
the battleship gray he chose
for the trim of his house—

maybe once a sailor
no family left

his only friends for years
the obedient Sammys

and now this Cindy
loyal enough behind fence
or leashed

but loath to resist an open door
with its possibility
of rabbit.

If the past is any measure
she will run awhile now,
follow scents that excite her

return to him when she stops
hearing her name.

# TIGER WIDOW

*First man, first tiger*
*born of one mother—*
*a human womb.*

*Man stays home*
*watches a village grow.*
*Tiger moves to forest.*

*One day man goes*
*into forest*
*fights his brother*

*lures tiger to a river*
*and with poisoned dart*
*slays him.*

*Tiger's bones gather*
*in the river's reeds*

*where Dingu-Aneni*
*brings forth from them*
*many tigers.*

I've hardly heard a story
without a tiger in it
eyes stony as fate:

*tiger god, tiger man*
*were-tiger.*

In folk tales, he listens
at hut's door, helps
the Rajah's son win a wife

joins the Milky Way
tries to eat moon or sun.

It is told that the Buddha
journeying toward nirvana
gave his own flesh
to a starved tigress mother.

My village knows this cat
as yours might know
serpent or wolf.

Here, by the Bay of Bengal
on the edge of the mangroves
man and tiger remain wary
fatal brothers:

Tigers coming into the village
are shot

yet always there are more
to destroy men entering forest
for fish, wood, or honey.

They were six hunting honey
the day my husband died.
I prayed six would return

offered petals at the shrine
of the crowned goddess.


Her crown toppled
three were killed.

They call us *tiger widows.*
We dress in mourning clothes
stare ahead with our own cold eyes.

They give us machines
to help us sew

but our children starve
despite our stitching.

Around the village I move
more softly now, lower my gaze
before our men

yet I hide something new in me
free and fierce:

Passing close to the mangroves
I've begun to hear their whisper.

*Wrap yourself in the striped shawl*
*of your wedding.*

*Walk in on quiet feet.*

*Become hunter.*

# WAITING ROOM

The seats fill with seniors
so many they seem to have come
for bargain day—

Tuesday special at the pancake house
or dollar store.

*You don't remember me*
one man says to another beside him.
*Tell me about yourself,*
*maybe I will—*

patients' murmur like static
a radio broadcasts between stations.

When a young woman enters
pulling a cart of drugs and gifts
her quick step stirs up winter's air.

*Hello, beautiful lady—*
the woman hunched in a wheelchair
extending an arm.

But the beautiful lady looks
down as she passes.

On business, in a hurry
she's at the reception
offering company brochures

totes, wall clocks, and pens
then sharing a laugh
before leaving the room

to resume its slow routine.
Sometimes an inner door opens.

Someone is called for examination
the drawing of blood.

Or someone comes out, to go home
with a list of new worries
a few sample pills.

Beside the closet of waiting coats
a century plant once spiny and firm shrivels
denied its small measure of water.

# MORPHINE

The hospital spins:
daylight and fluorescence
tumble with shadows

mumbling, shuffling

whispers of tubes
and their fluids of sugar and salt.


From the next bed
a woman calls softly for Jesus
and night comes with its own
metronome:

the beeping of an empty pump
a scream
then silence takes a turn.


On the window's black screen
a plane rises
like an aberrant heartbeat

and when darkness slips in
to kiss a hand
it leaves a bruise
the color of its lips.

# APRIL, DARK SHADOW

An April robin bats head
and breast against our window
to guard his chosen home
from his own reflection—

Don Quixote, self-appointed
old knight, tilting at our pane.

Inside the house: winged shadow.

\*

The lush season: rush of cells
to multiply—

stem, petal, leaf
the bird expanding beyond its shell.

For some, in the body
a darker bloom:
shadow on liver or lung

those cells, too, rampant
with the urge for division.

\*

Against the hospital's
radiant windows, each patient
is a silhouette

and the silent orderly
moves like night's shadow

barely noticed
as he waits outside doors
with his vacant gurney

to take the ill
where they need to go.

*

Clock to clock to watch
with its jeweled balance

on the designated April morning
we tap buttons, turn stems
to make the days lighter

and age an hour in the minutes it takes
to move digits and hands.

# WHISPER SONG

What began so musically
in the spring ends as a whisper.
Some birds…sing their regular songs
with their beaks closed, or very
quietly from cover in trees.
— E. Duensing, A. G. Millmoss


Unsteady, language.
Fatigue or age erases words
and the voice once strong
loses tone.

Yet the couple awaken
at the same moment
often in separate rooms

smile together on invisible
inaudible cue.

We bend closer
to follow their speech
as they withdraw

into a strangeness
where fragments of light
once entangled

continue their dance for two
a universe apart.

But all we catch—
shoes muddied, ears still tuned
to cricket and bird—
is the whisper of their departure:

the muffled yes or no
a story from the past
told many times before—

familiar notes once bold
earthy in aim, quiet now
hummed for the self
beak closed.

# SORTING

Questions pile up fast
as the boxes to give away—

where did you go

in the black gown
whose waist is cinched
with satin?

the Mexican serapes
saffron and rose?

This chore
we should have shared—
packed past with story.

Alone, no memory
of these shoes or shirts

I tie up effects
of a stranger

for other strangers
who will mark
your laundered cottons
with their sweat.

Still the closets
tell on you—vague tales

about elegance
that was not easy
called for mistakes

like photography's
discarded shots before
the perfect portrait.

About someone
who held on to old sizes
shapes and colors

hoping perhaps
to return one day to youth

as I held off
before the packing up
in case you came back to us
requiring clothes.

# THE KITCHEN TABLE

after Jean Siméon Chardin

Because the earth has given
everything

from grape to bird
to copper and wood

the palette, too, is earth's—
warmed here by the late sun

of supper time. Hours
since family left

after a Sunday visit
whose aroma hangs on—
onion, carrot, pheasant stewed
in the pot with unseated lid.

The widower has poured
his evening wine, placed cheese
bread, eggs within his reach

then stepped into his garden
to cut greens
for his day's last meal.

Inside the kitchen, shadows begin
to fill the empty carafe

stain a knife, blade
pointed toward the white cloth
that still holds the pheasant's bones

and drapes over table's edge
like two robed figures
bowed low at this altar

sorrowed by so much lost
hungry for what remains.

# ACKNOWLEDGMENTS

A heartfelt thank-you to the many teachers, workshop mates, and friends who have helped me with encouragement and suggestions during the years these poems were written, particularly Milica Banjanin, Sarah Cotterill, Gloria Hammack, Judith Harris, Sanford Leikin, Stephanie Siciarz, and Judith Whiton. To my husband André, special love and gratitude for believing in my poetic efforts even while refraining from comment on any poem for fear of hurting my feelings. He is a good man.

I would also like to express appreciation to the following literary magazines that originally published poems included in this volume:

*The Cape Rock* ("Firewater," "Saguaro")
*Heliotrope* ("Black Balloon," "Morphine")
*Peregrine* ("Riding Lesson")
*River Oak Review* ("Meditation")
*Sulphur River Literary Review* ("Three Elephants," "A River Back," "Siltstone")
*Wayne Literary Review* ("Tiger Widow")
*Willow Review* ("House Sparrows")

"Broadkill Beach" originally appeared in *Mercy of Tides: Poems for a Beach House* (Margot Wizansky, ed.), Salt Marsh Pottery Press (S. Dartmouth, MA), 2003.

"November Passage" originally appeared in *Rough Places Plain: Poems of the Mountains* (Margot Wizansky, ed.), Salt Marsh Pottery Press, 2005.

References for epigraphs and quotations:

- Book epigraph and "Whisper Song." E. Duensing, A. G. Millmoss: *Backyard and Beyond: A Guide for Discovering the Outdoors.* Golden CO, Fulcrum Publishing, 1992.
- "Meditation." Wang Wei: "At the Hermitage of Master Fu." In: *Midnight Flute: Chinese Poems of Love and Longing* (Sam Hamill, trans.). Boston, London, Shambhala, 1994.
- "Evidence for Strings." Brian Greene: *The Elegant Universe.* New York, Vintage Books, 1999.
- "Soul of Water." Gaston Bachelard: *The Psychoanalysis of Fire* (Alan C. M. Ross, trans.). Boston, Beacon Press, 1964.
- "Planting Tulips." Anna Pavord: *The Tulip: The Story of a Flower That Has Made Men Mad.* New York, London, Bloomsbury Publishing, 1999.
- "Ruby." George Frederick Kunz: *The Curious Lore of Precious Stones.* New York, Dover Publications, Inc., 1971, originally published 1913.
- "The Old House." Carl Sandburg: "Prairie" In: *Cornhuskers,* 1918.

- "Bonnard's Peaches." Quotation within poem is from Antoine Terrasse: *Bonnard: Shimmering Color* (L. Hirsch, trans.). New York, Abrams, 2000.
- "Flat Run." *Scattering Dust, Slinging Flame*, manuscript by Gloria M. Hammack.

# ABOUT THE AUTHOR

Dee LeRoy's poems have appeared in numerous literary magazines and in two anthologies. *Earthbound* is her first collection. A retired science writer and editor, she lives in Maryland.

leroy.earthbound@gmail.com

Made in the USA
Middletown, DE
20 April 2019